SPEECH IMPROVEMENT REPRODUCIBLE MASTERS

(REVISED)

g-g-g-g-g-g-g-g

la-la-la-la-la

m-m-m-m-m-m-m

Written by Jean Gilliam DeGaetano

Great Ideas for Teaching, Inc. • P.O. Box 444 • Wrightsville Beach, NC • 28480

ISBN 1-886143-51-X

Speech Improvement
Reproducible Masters (Revised)

By Jean Gilliam DeGaetano

Introduction:

Learning to improve speech should be a pleasant experience for the child. It is with this philosophy in mind that this set of reproducible masters is designed. Materials, while functional, also should be attractive and geared to a child's level of interest and ability. However, preparing such items is a most time-consuming job for the therapist. The purpose of **Speech Improvement Reproducible Masters** is to make the therapist's work easier by allowing him/her to produce inexpensively as many copies of each sheet as needed. The materials can then be given to all the children to keep and to practice at home. Additionally, the worksheets made from these masters will serve as an aid to parents who, in most cases, desire to help their children but lack the knowledge to correct speech errors.

Page 1 for each sound describes how the sound is made. It is intended to teach the child and inform his/her parents as to how to use the speech mechanisms to produce the sound. Page 2 of each sound set contains pictures and words with the sound in the beginning, medial, and final positions. Page 3 presents an entertaining activity through which the child can use the speech sound in sentences.

Suggestions for Using the Masters:

Page 1 for each sound describes how to produce the sound and tells whether or not the voice is used. After the instructor has read the directions to the child, the instructor and the child, using a mirror, should work together on the production of the sound. After the sound is produced successfully in isolation, it should be used with the vowels at the bottom of page 1. This page, if sent home, serves the dual purpose of teaching the parents as well as teaching the child.

Suggestions for varying page 1:

1. Ask the child if he/she can produce the sound by a negative method. For example, on (p), ask him/her if he/she can make a (p) sound without closing his lips. Have the child try in front of a mirror to produce (p) with his/her mouth open. When he/she cannot, again go over the proper directions. This time he/she will realize the importance of closing his lips.

2. Play a listening game with the sound. Say the child's sound with one other sound. The sounds may be repeated in any order. Draw a circle for the child and one for yourself. These will serve as faces. As the child says his/her sound, he/she will fill in, one at a time, the eyes, the nose, the mouth, and the ears. If he/she makes an error, you draw the feature on your paper. The first face completed signifies a winner.

Page 2 presents the sound in the three positions in words. The names of the pictures should be practiced aloud.

Suggestions for varying page 2:

1. Mispronounce the word. Ask the child to listen and correct the error. For example, on (sh), you may ask, "Do you see a chip?" The child should reply, "No I don't see a chip, but I see a ship." This game can be played with all the words on page 2.

2. Put numbers 1, 2, 3, 4 and 5 on paper squares and either fold the square or turn them face down on a table. The child takes a number and must tell that number of things about a picture. For example, the child might get "2" on "ship." He/she must then tell two things about a ship, such as, "A ship sails in water, and a ship has an anchor."

3. Cut out the pictures to use in this game. Three paper cups are needed. Put a number (1, 2, or 3) on the bottom of each cup. A picture is hidden under one cup. If a shoe is hidden, for instance, the person hiding it would say, "I have hidden a shoe." The other player might ask, "Is the shoe under cup 2?" If it is not found in two guesses, the same person hides it again. If it is found, the other person takes a turn hiding it. Increase the number of cups as you increase the number of players. This will also increase the number of guesses.

Page 3 is an activity sheet to encourage the child to use the correct sound in conversation. Directions are given on page 3 of each sound set.

Suggestions for varying page 3:

1. After having the child perform the activity once for practice, let him repeat it. This time use a tape recorder. Play the tape back for him/her to hear.

2. Have the child pretend he/she cannot produce the sound correctly, and record the activity again, with the sound in error. Play this tape back and compare it to the correct recording.

3. The child may like to have the recording containing the error erased and another correct recording made in its place.

(B) is the "bubbling sound." Close your lips lightly. As you open your lips, let a little puff of air escape. Use your voice.

If you do not close your lips, you may hear the (v) sound. Practice in front of a mirror to make sure you close your lips.

Say:

bay,	bay,	bay,	bay,	bay,	bay
bee,	bee,	bee,	bee,	bee,	bee
bie,	bie,	bie,	bie,	bie,	bie
bow,	bow,	bow,	bow,	bow,	bow
boo,	boo,	boo,	boo,	boo,	boo

Sometimes (b) is at the beginning of a word.

bus   ball   bird

Sometimes (b) is in the middle of a word.

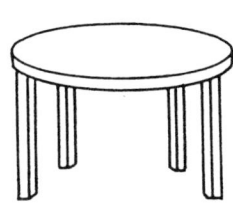

table   mailbox   rabbit

Sometimes (b) is at the end of a word.

doorknob   web   crab

Say the name of each picture aloud.

Name the things that are in Betty's bubbles.

Say: "Betty's bubble has a _____."

Color the pictures.

Great Ideas for Teaching, Inc.

Speech Improvement
Reproducible Masters (Revised)

(D) is the "drum sound." Open your mouth lightly and touch your tongue tip to the bony ridge behind your upper front teeth. Let a small burst of air push the tongue tip away from the gum ridge. Use your voice.

Pretend you are a drum and say:

dum - d - d - dum - d - d - dum - dum - dum.

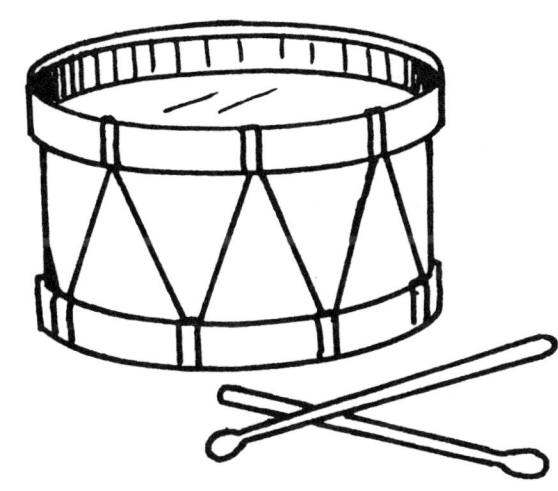

Say: day, day, day, day, day, day
dee, dee, dee, dee, dee, dee
die, die, die, die, die, die
doe, doe, doe, doe, doe, doe
do, do, do, do, do, do

Great Ideas for Teaching, Inc.

Speech Improvement
Reproducible Masters (Revised)

Sometimes (d) is at the beginning of a word.

| door | duck | dog |

Sometimes (d) is in the middle of a word.

| ladder | window | spider |

Sometimes (d) is at the end of a word.

| bed | head | bread |

Say the name of each picture aloud.

Dodi wants to hide something behind the door.

Cut the five pictures apart, and cut the door as marked. One player places a picture behind the door. The other players in turn must guess what it is and ask, "Does Dodi have a _____ behind the door?" The answer should be, "No, Dodi does not have a _____." or "Yes, Dodi has a _____." The player who guesses correctly hides the next picture.

(F) is the sound a cat makes when it sees a big dog coming near. Touch your top front teeth lightly to your lower lip. Now blow out air. Put your hand under the front of your chin, and you can feel the air come out and down. Do not use your voice. Look in a mirror and try to say: "f-f-f-f-f-f-f-f-f-f."

Say: fay, fay, fay, fay, fay, fay

fee, fee, fee, fee, fee, fee

fie, fie, fie, fie, fie, fie

foe, foe, foe, foe, foe, foe

foo, foo, foo, foo, foo, foo

Speech Improvement
Reproducible Masters (Revised)

Sometimes (f) is at the beginning of a word.

fish

four

finger

Sometimes (f) is in the middle of a word.

ruffles

daffodil

coffee

Sometimes (f) is at the end of a word.

leaf

hoof

roof

Say the name of each picture aloud.

A funny fish went fishing and caught many things. Cut out all the fish and turn them face down on a table. As you pick up each one, say, "A funny fish went fishing and caught a _____." (You might also put three staples in each fish and "go fishing" with a magnet.)

(G) is the "frog sound" made deep in your throat. You must open your mouth slightly and use your voice. Put your hand flat against your throat. Can you feel the "frog sound" when you say, "ung-guh, ung-guh?"

Say:
gay,	gay,	gay,	gay,	gay,	gay
gee,	gee,	gee,	gee,	gee,	gee
guy,	guy,	guy,	guy,	guy,	guy
go,	go,	go,	go,	go,	go
goo,	goo,	goo,	goo,	goo,	goo

Speech Improvement
Reproducible Masters (Revised)

Sometimes (g) is at the beginning of a word.

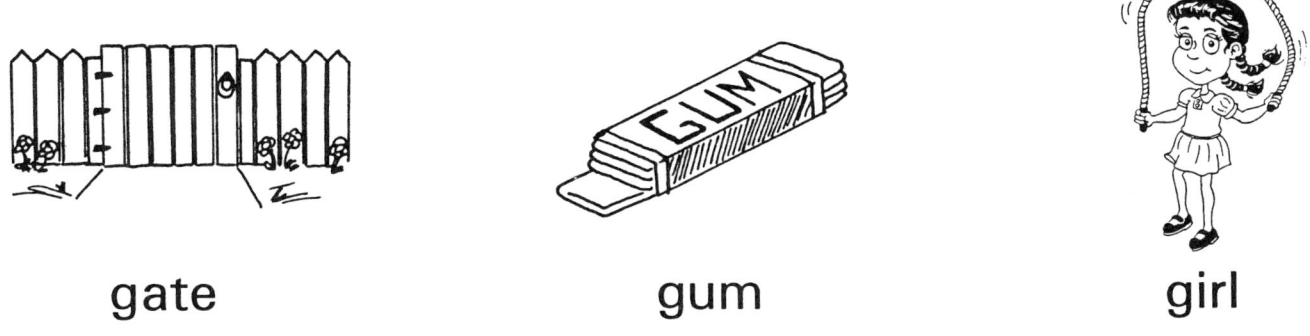

gate   gum   girl

Sometimes (g) is in the middle of a word.

wagon   tiger   sugar

Sometimes (g) is at the end of a word.

rug   bug   pig

Say the name of each picture aloud.

Cut out all the squares and paste each one in the center of a 2½-inch cardboard square. Spread out the squares face down on a table. One player turns up two cards. He says, "Gabby Goat has a _____ and a _____." If the cards are alike, he removes them from the table and takes another turn. If they are not alike, he turns them face down again. The object is to remember where all the cards are and to find the matching pairs. The player with the most pairs wins.

gate	gate	gas pump	gas pump	girl
pig	pig	gum	gum	girl
bug	bug	wagon	wagon	hot dog
dog	dog	goggles	goggles	hot dog

Speech Improvement
Reproducible Masters (Revised)

(J) is the "jet sound." The tongue tip should lightly touch the bony ridge behind your upper front teeth. Your tongue tip will hold back the air until you release it by lowering the tip and allowing the air to explode. Use your voice.

Your "teeth gate" must be closed when you start to make this sound.

Say: jay, jay, jay, jay, jay, jay
      jee, jee, jee, jee, jee, jee
      jie, jie, jie, jie, jie, jie
      joe, joe, joe, joe, joe, joe
      joo, joo, joo, joo, joo, joo

Sometimes (j) is at the beginning of a word.

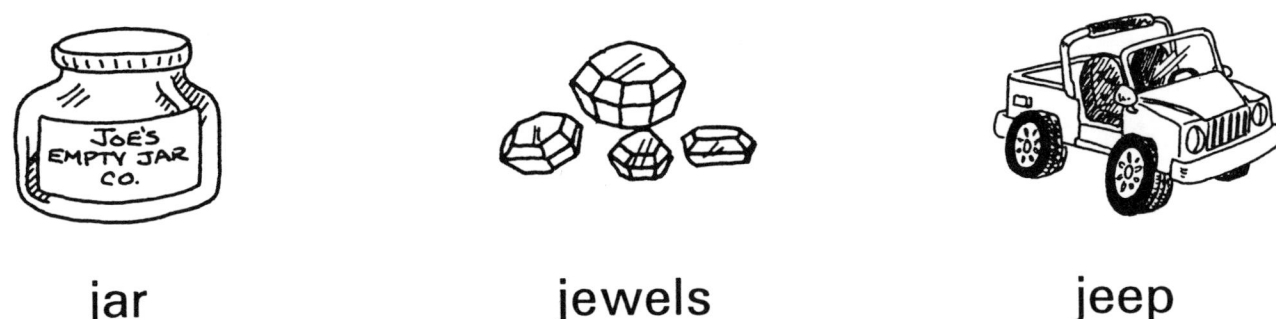

| jar | jewels | jeep |

Sometimes (j) is in the middle of a word.

| magic | engine | angel |
| (j) | (j) | (j) |

Sometimes (j) is at the end of a word.

| bridge | garbage | cage |
| (j) | (j) | (j) |

Say the name of each picture aloud.

Draw a line to the picture that completes each
sentence. Say the sentence aloud.

On my bread I put butter and _____.   jug

A boy puts on his _____.   orange
(j)

I will eat a juicy _____.   jam

The bear is in a _____.   jacket

The soldier rode in a _____.   cage
(j)

Water is in a _____.   giant
(j)

Jack ran when he saw the _____.   jeep

(K) or (c) is the "old hen's sound." The sound comes from the back of your throat. Pull back your tongue to close the "tunnel" to your throat. Let the sound escape with a slight exploding of air. Do not use your voice.

Look in a mirror. The skin at the top of your throat will "puff out" like the old hen's when you say: "k, c, k, c, k, c, k."

k-c-k-c-k-c-k-c-k-c-k

Say:
kay,	kay,	kay,	kay,	kay,	kay
kee,	kee,	kee,	kee,	kee,	kee
kie,	kie,	kie,	kie,	kie,	kie
coe,	coe,	coe,	coe,	coe,	coe
coo,	coo,	coo,	coo,	coo,	coo

Speech Improvement
Reproducible Masters (Revised)

Sometimes (k,c) is at the beginning of a word.

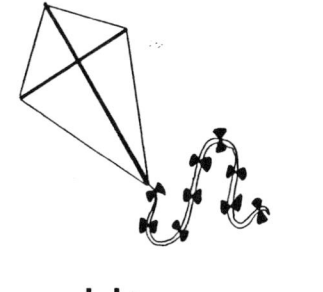

kite

cap

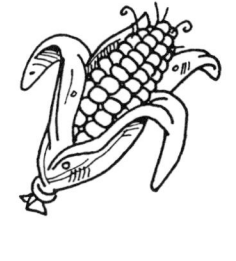

corn

Sometimes (k,c) is in the middle of a word.

pumpkin

acorn

monkey

Sometimes (k,c) is at the end of a word.

book

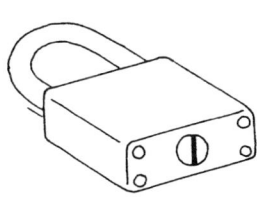

lock

duck

Say the name of each picture aloud.

Color everything that tastes sweet. Draw a line
under everything that is not sweet.

Connie is having a picnic. She wants to pack a
nice lunch. Circle all the things you think Connie
should put in the picnic basket.

Say: "Connie can take _____ on her picnic."

cake

candy

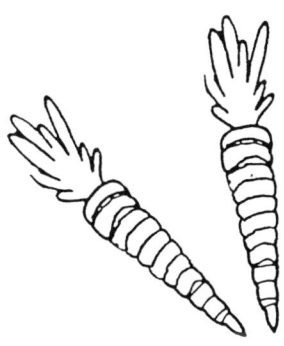

carrots

cabbage

corn

cookies

Speech Improvement
Reproducible Masters (Revised)

(L) is the "singing sound." Your tongue tip should lightly touch the bony ridge behind your upper front teeth. Use your voice.

Say: "la-la-la-la." Look in the mirror. Did your tongue come popping out? Do not hit your teeth with your tongue tip.

Say: | lay, | lay, | lay, | lay, | lay, | lay
|---|---|---|---|---|---|
| lee, | lee, | lee, | lee, | lee, | lee |
| lie, | lie, | lie, | lie, | lie, | lie |
| low, | low, | low, | low, | low, | low |
| loo, | loo, | loo, | loo, | loo, | loo |

Great Ideas for Teaching, Inc.

Speech Improvement
Reproducible Masters (Revised)

Sometimes (l) is at the beginning of a word.

leg

lamp

leaf

Sometimes (l) is in the middle of a word.

sailor

balloon

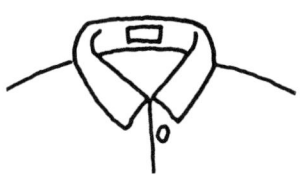

collar

Sometimes (l) is at the end of a word.

ball

bell

pencil

Say the name of each picture aloud.

Color each lollipop the color of the flavor you like.

As you color each lollipop, say, "I would like a

_____ lollipop. I will color it_____."
(flavor)   (color)

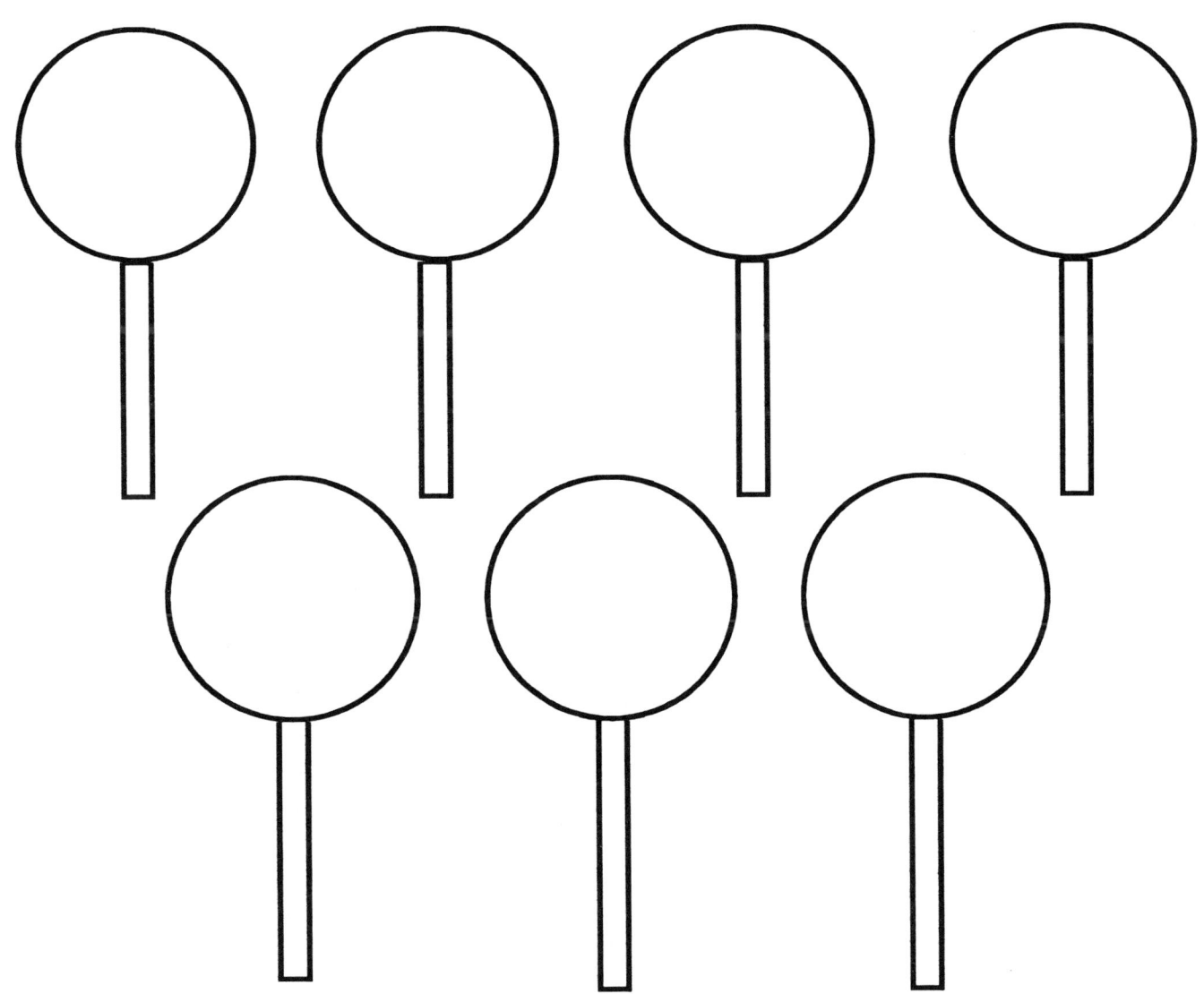

(M) is the "m-m-m, m-m-m good sound" you say when you finish eating your favorite piece of candy.

Close your lips lightly and let the sound come through your nose. Use your voice.

If you hold your nose closed, you cannot make the m-m-m-m sound. Try it. The sound must come through your nose.

m-m-m-m-m-m-m

Say: may, may, may, may, may, may

me, me, me, me, me, me

my, my, my, my, my, my

mow, mow, mow, mow, mow, mow

moo, moo, moo, moo, moo, moo

Speech Improvement
Reproducible Masters (Revised)

Sometimes (m) is at the beginning of a word.

| milk | mittens | monkey |

Sometimes (m) is in the middle of a word.

| hammer | tomato | camel |

Sometimes (m) is at the end of a word.

| home | comb | ice cream |

Say the name of each picture aloud.

Speech Improvement
Reproducible Masters (Revised)

Mr. Monkey is holding a mitten. You can find out what he has in the mitten if you will do this: (1) Cut out the circle in Mr. Monkey's mitten. (2) Cut out the object wheel, and place it behind Mr. Monkey's hands. (3) Match the dot at the center of the wheel with the dot over Mr. Monkey's hands, and attach the wheel with a brass fastener.

As you turn the wheel, say: "Mr. Monkey has _____ in his mitten."

Speech Improvement
Reproducible Masters (Revised)

(N) is the "vibrating nose sound." Lightly touch your tongue tip to the bony gum ridge behind your upper front teeth. Now, use your voice. Put your fingers on the bridge of your nose, and you will feel the humming vibrations.

Air comes through your nostrils when you say this sound.

Say: nay, nay, nay, nay, nay, nay
      nee, nee, nee, nee, nee, nee
      nie, nie, nie, nie, nie, nie
      no,   no,   no,   no,   no,   no
      noo, noo, noo, noo, noo, noo

Speech Improvement
Reproducible Masters (Revised)

Sometimes (n) is at the beginning of a word.

needle   nine   nail

Sometimes (n) is in the middle of a word.

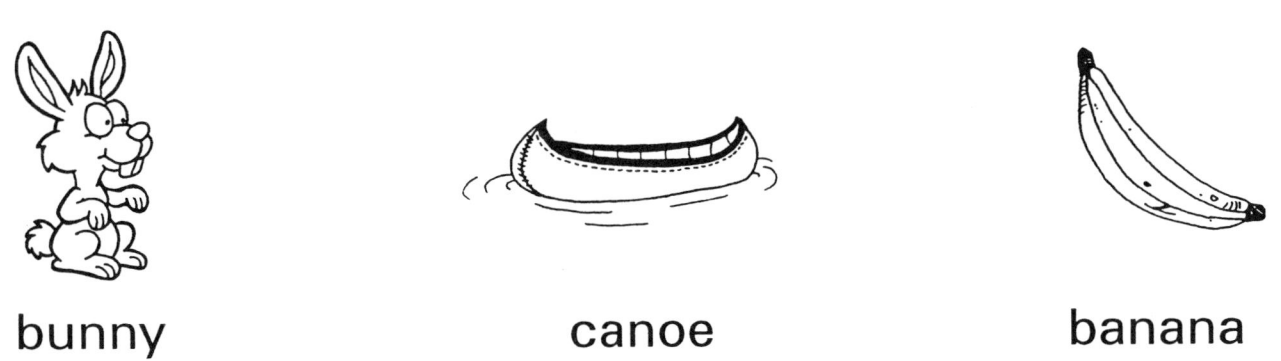

bunny   canoe   banana

Sometimes (n) is at the end of a word.

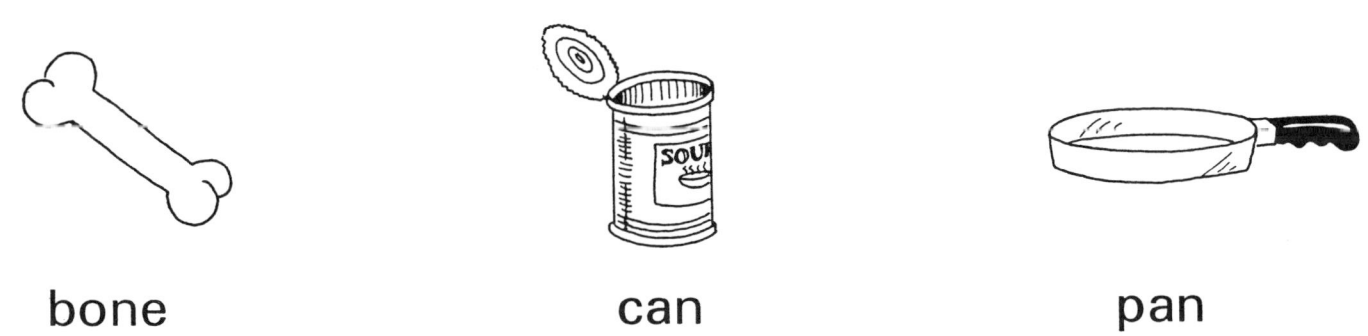

bone   can   pan

Say the name of each picture aloud.

Put a line under each of the things whose name hums in your nose when you say it. Color orange everything whose name does not hum.

Say: _____ hums in my nose. (Touch the bridge of your nose lightly to feel the hum.)

9

nine

nut

needle

nurse

bear

cat

nest

nail

fish

note

Speech Improvement
Reproducible Masters (Revised)

(P) is the "popping sound." Close your lips lightly. As you open your lips, let a puff of air "explode" out. Do not use your voice.

p-p-p-p-p-p-p-p-p-p

Hold a small strip of paper about two inches from your lips. It should "pop out" when you say these sounds.

Say:
pay,	pay,	pay,	pay,	pay,	pay
pea,	pea,	pea,	pea,	pea,	pea
pie,	pie,	pie,	pie,	pie,	pie
poe,	poe,	poe,	poe,	poe,	poe
poo,	poo,	poo,	poo,	poo,	poo

Speech Improvement
Reproducible Masters (Revised)

Sometimes (p) is at the beginning of a word.

pie   pail   pot

Sometimes (p) is in the middle of a word.

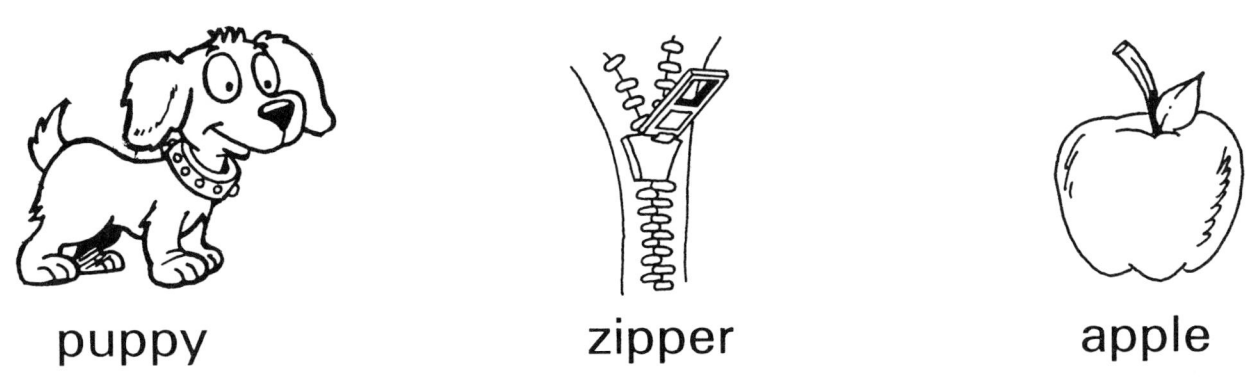

puppy   zipper   apple

Sometimes (p) is at the end of a word.

cap   lamp   cup

Say the name of each picture aloud.

Name the things Penny can put into a pie.

Say: "Penny can put _____ into a pie."

Name the things Penny cannot put into a pie.

Say: "Penny cannot put _____ into a pie."

a peach

a lollipop

a pencil

an apple

a mop

a pumpkin

Speech Improvement
Reproducible Masters (Revised)

(R) is the "fire engine sound." You must slightly curl up the tip of your tongue as you pull the entire tongue back a little. Be careful not to round your lips too much, or you will hear the (w) sound. Use your voice.

Pretend you are a fire engine rushing to a fire. Turn on your siren.

r-r-r-r-r-r-r-r-r-r-r-r-r-r-r-r-r

Say:	ray,	ray,	ray,	ray,	ray,	ray
	ree,	ree,	ree,	ree,	ree,	ree
	rye,	rye,	rye,	rye,	rye,	rye
	row,	row,	row,	row,	row,	row
	roo,	roo,	roo,	roo,	roo,	roo

Sometimes (r) is at the beginning of a word.

ring   radio   rooster

Sometimes (r) is in the middle of a word.

carrot   cherries   fairy

Sometimes (r) is at the end of a word.

ear   fire   four

Say the name of each picture aloud.

Circle all the things that would be ruined if you left them out in the rain. Color red the things that would not be ruined.

rocket

roof

ring

rooster

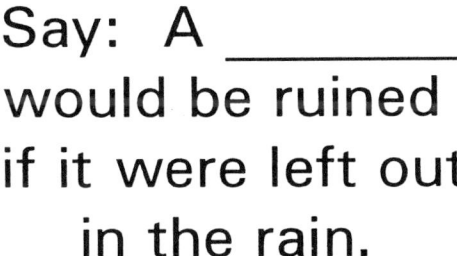

Say: A _____ would be ruined if it were left out in the rain.

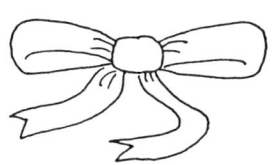

ribbon

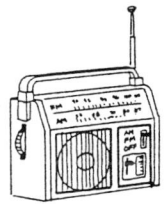

radio

rabbit

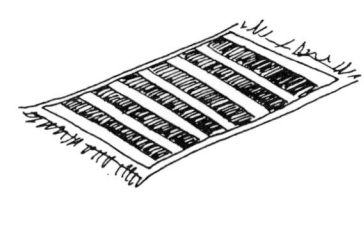

rug

Speech Improvement
Reproducible Masters (Revised)

(S) is the "snake sound." Close your teeth as you do when you smile. Be sure to hide your tongue behind your teeth. The "snake sound" must come from between your tongue and your front teeth, not from the sides of your mouth. Do not use your voice.

Hiss gently: "s-s-s-s-s-s   s-s-s-s-s-s." (If your tongue tip slips out, you do not have your teeth closed.)

Say:

say,	say,	say,	say,	say,	say
see,	see,	see,	see,	see,	see
sigh,	sigh,	sigh,	sigh,	sigh,	sigh
so,	so,	so,	so,	so,	so
sue,	sue,	sue,	sue,	sue,	sue

Speech Improvement
Reproducible Masters (Revised)

Sometimes (s) is at the beginning of a word.

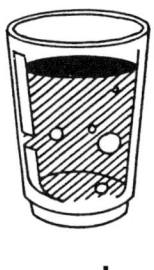

soda

sandwich

sun

Sometimes (s) is in the middle of a word.

baseball

bicycle
(s)

lasso

Sometimes (s) is at the end of a word.

mouse

bus

gas

Say the name of each picture aloud.

Cut out both circles. With a brass fastener, attach the center dots together with circle #1 on top of circle #2. Turn the top circle so Sammy Snake can see each picture.

Say: "Sammy Snake sees a _____."

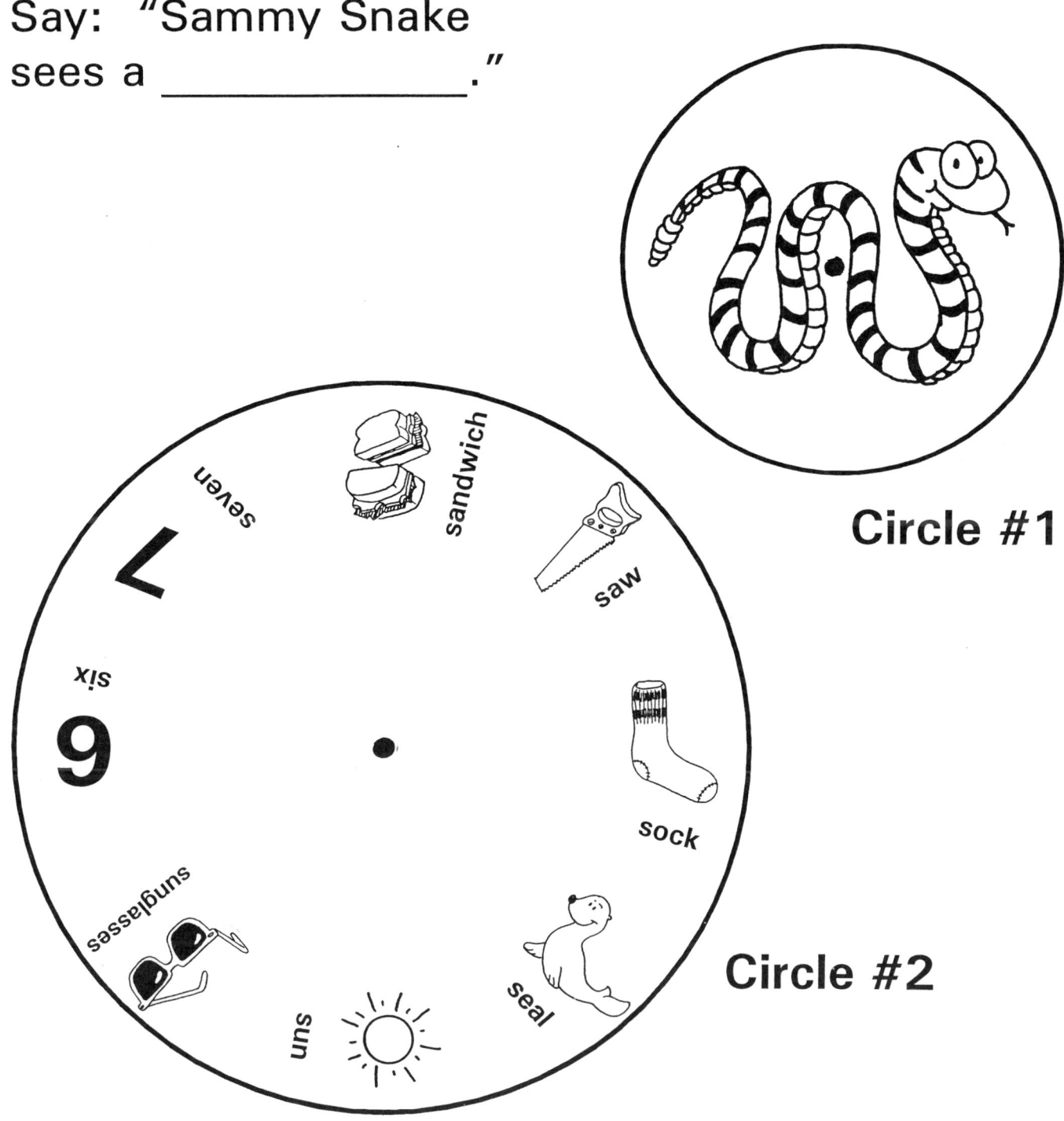

Circle #1

Circle #2

Speech Improvement
Reproducible Masters (Revised)

(T) is the "clock-ticking sound." Lightly touch your tongue tip to the bony ridge behind your upper front teeth. You must open your mouth slightly, but do not use your voice. (T) is a voiceless sound.

Be careful not to hit your teeth with your tongue tip.

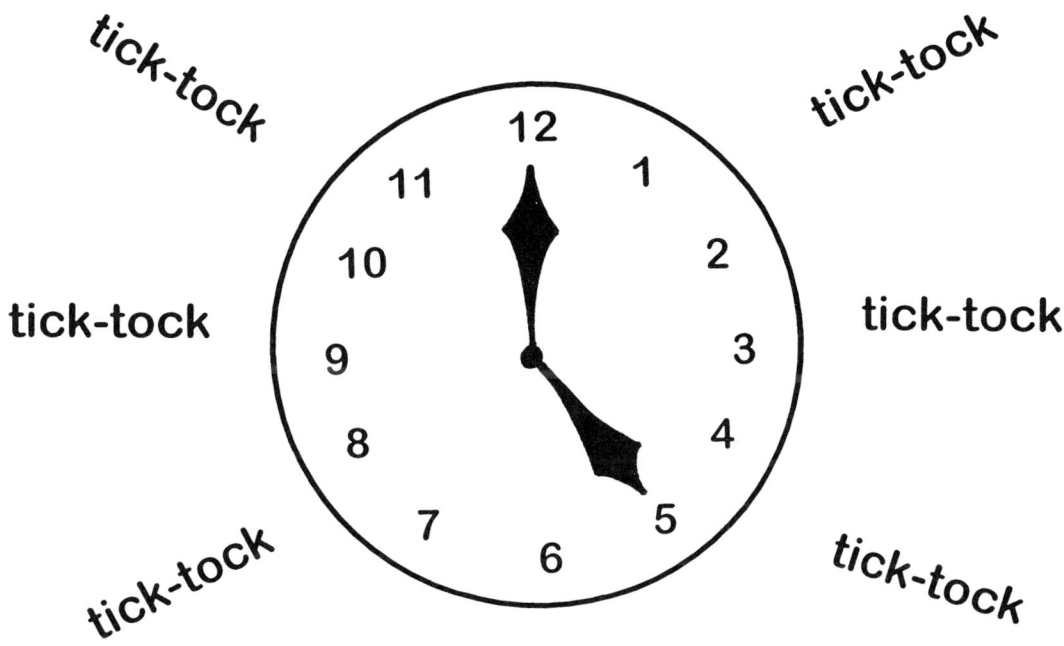

Say:

tay,	tay,	tay,	tay,	tay,	tay
tee,	tee,	tee,	tee,	tee,	tee
tie,	tie,	tie,	tie,	tie,	tie
toe,	toe,	toe,	toe,	toe,	toe
too,	too,	too,	too,	too,	too

Speech Improvement
Reproducible Masters (Revised)

Sometimes (t) is at the beginning of a word.

tie	top	toes

Sometimes (t) is in the middle of a word.

mitten	bottle	butter

Sometimes (t) is at the end of a word.

heart	hat	pot

Say the name of each picture aloud.

Speech Improvement
Reproducible Masters (Revised)

Tippy has a new toy box. Tippy's mother told Tippy to put only toys in her toy box. If you are a good listener, you will be able to help Tippy put things in her new toy box.

Color each picture that belongs in the toy box, and say: "Tippy can put a _____ in her new toy box."

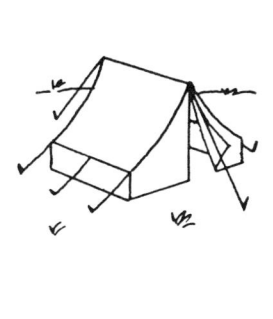

tent

top

bat

toy telephone

toy truck

toy boat

table

toy tank

turtle

toy tractor

Speech Improvement
Reproducible Masters (Revised)

(V) is the "motor sound." Touch your upper front teeth lightly to your bottom lip. Look in a mirror when you practice this sound. Use your voice.

Pretend you are a vacuum cleaner. Say: v-v-v-v-v-v-v-v-v-v-v-v-v-v. Cup your hand under your mouth, and you can feel a flow of air when your motor is running.

Say:
vay,	vay,	vay,	vay,	vay,	vay
vee,	vee,	vee,	vee,	vee,	vee
vie,	vie,	vie,	vie,	vie,	vie
voe,	voe,	voe,	voe,	voe,	voe
voo,	voo,	voo,	voo,	voo,	voo

Sometimes (v) is at the beginning of a word.

vase   valentine   vest

Sometimes (v) is in the middle of a word.

television   seven   shovel

Sometimes (v) is at the end of a word.

stove   five   sleeve

Say the name of each picture aloud.

Victor and Vinnie are looking at a television set. Cut out the individual pictures in the picture strips. Place each picture on the blank screen.

Say: Victor and Vinnie see a _____ on their television (or TV) set.

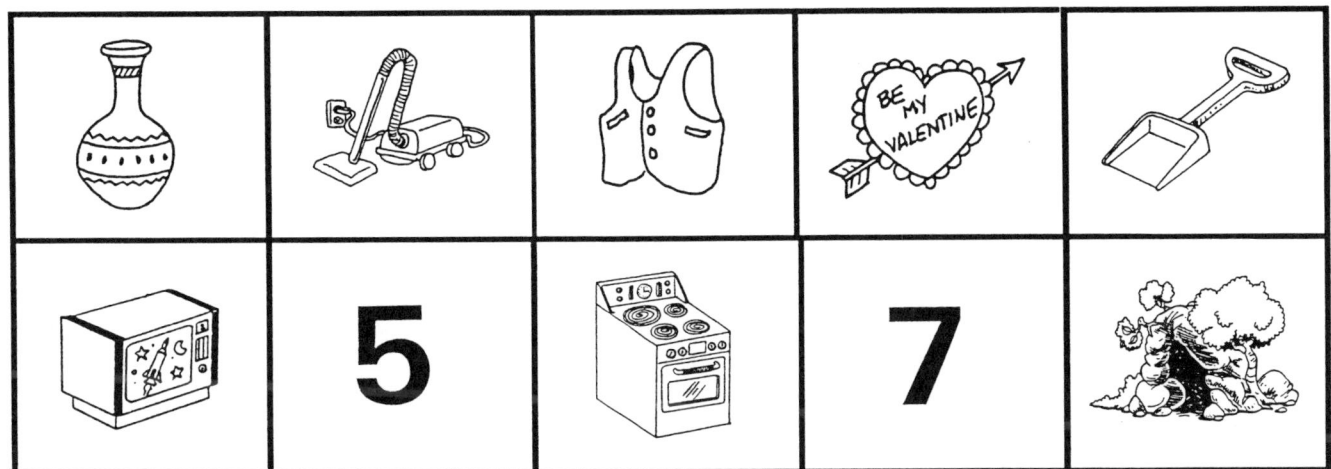

Speech Improvement
Reproducible Masters (Revised)

(Z) is the "buzzing sound." Close your teeth as you do when you smile. Be sure to hide your tongue tip behind your teeth. (Z) is made very much like the (s) sound except you must use your voice to make a buzzing sound.

Pretend you are a bee diving for a target.

Buzz-z-z-z-z-z-z-z-z-z.

Say:	zay,	zay,	zay,	zay,	zay,	zay
	zee,	zee,	zee,	zee,	zee,	zee
	zie,	zie,	zie,	zie,	zie,	zie
	zoe,	zoe,	zoe,	zoe,	zoe,	zoe
	zoo,	zoo,	zoo,	zoo,	zoo,	zoo

Speech Improvement
Reproducible Masters (Revised)

Sometimes (z) is at the beginning of a word.

zipper   zero   zebra

Sometimes (z) is in the middle of a word.

razor   music   buzzer
                (z)

Sometimes (z) is at the end of a word.

eyes   bees   cheese
(z)   (z)   (z)

Say the name of each picture aloud.

Speech Improvement
Reproducible Masters (Revised)

Zizzy hides when he hears something buzzing.

Color each thing you think can buzz.

Say: "Zizzy, hide! A _____ can buzz-z-z, buzz-z-z, buzz."

Mark out each thing that cannot buzz.

Say: "Zizzy, come out! A _____ cannot buzz-z-z, buzz-z-z, buzz."

mosquito

mouse

horsefly

honeybee

dog

cat

fly

duck

hornet

Speech Improvement
Reproducible Masters (Revised)

(Ch) is the "sneezy sound." Extend your lips a little in a slightly rounded position. When starting the sound, close the mouth opening with your teeth. Do not use your voice. The tongue tip should be a little behind the bony ridge back of your upper front teeth. Air "explodes" when the tongue tip is lowered.

Pretend someone sprinkles pepper on your nose and you sneeze, "Ah-choo, ah-choo, ah-choo."

Say: chay, chay, chay, chay, chay, chay
      chee, chee, chee, chee, chee, chee
      chie, chie, chie, chie, chie, chie
      choe, choe, choe, choe, choe, choe
      chew, chew, chew, chew, chew, chew

Speech Improvement
Reproducible Masters (Revised)

Sometimes (ch) is at the beginning of a word.

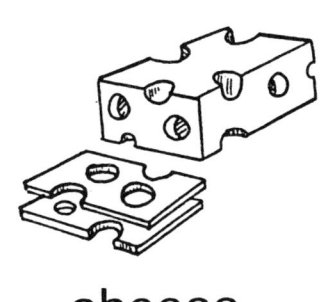 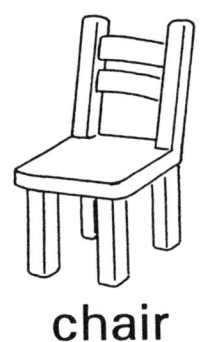 

cheese   chair   church

Sometimes (ch) is in the middle of a word.

pitcher   teacher   hatchet

Sometimes (ch) is at the end of a word.

watch   peach   witch

Say the name of each picture aloud.

Chubby Chucky's cheeks are puffed out because he is chewing a mouthful of food.

Cut out the circle above Chubby Chucky's paws. Then cut out the food wheel, and place the food behind Chucky. Match the dot at the center of the wheel with the dot on Chubby Chucky's nose. Attach the wheel with a brass fastener.

As you turn the wheel, say: "Chubby Chucky is chewing on _____."

Speech Improvement
Reproducible Masters (Revised)

(Sh) is the "big quiet sound." You must round your lips and close the mouth opening with your teeth. Now "shoosh" out air. The air must come out the front, not the sides, of your mouth.

Pretend you are telling someone to be quiet. Do not use your voice. Use only air. Say: "sh-sh-sh-sh-sh-sh sh-sh-sh-sh-sh-sh."

Say: shay,   shay,   shay,   shay,   shay,   shay
       she,   she,   she,   she,   she,   she
       shy,   shy,   shy,   shy,   shy,   shy
       show,   show,   show,   show,   show,   show
       shoe,   shoe,   shoe,   shoe,   shoe,   shoe

Sometimes (sh) is at the beginning of a word.

| shovel | ship | shoe |

Sometimes (sh) is in the middle of a word.

| dishes | mushroom | eggshell |

Sometimes (sh) is at the end of a word.

| fish | bush | dish |

Say the name of each picture aloud.

Speech Improvement
Reproducible Masters (Revised)

Fill in the things you would like to eat.

Say: "I wish I had a dish of _____ to eat."

sherbet

mushrooms

fish

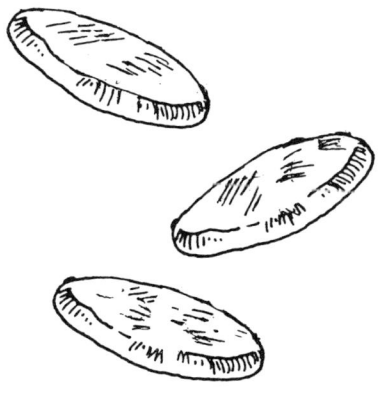

sugar cookies

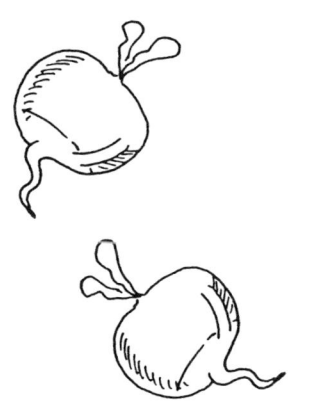

radishes

marshmallows

Speech Improvement
Reproducible Masters (Revised)

(Th) is the "stick-out-your-tongue sound" because it is the only sound that should show your tongue tip.

Open your mouth slightly. Place the tip of your tongue between your upper and lower teeth. Let a small burst of air escape as you pull your tongue tip back.

In some words, the (th) sound is voiceless. In other words, the voice is used for the (th) sound.

Say: thay,   thay,   thay,   thay,   thay,   thay
     thee,   thee,   thee,   thee,   thee,   thee
     thie,   thie,   thie,   thie,   thie,   thie
     thoe,   thoe,   thoe,   thoe,   thoe,   thoe
     thoo,   thoo,   thoo,   thoo,   thoo,   thoo

Speech Improvement
Reproducible Masters (Revised)

Sometimes (th) is at the beginning of a word.

thumb   three   thermos

Sometimes (th) is in the middle of a word.

toothbrush   bathtub   birthday cake

Sometimes (th) is at the end of a word.

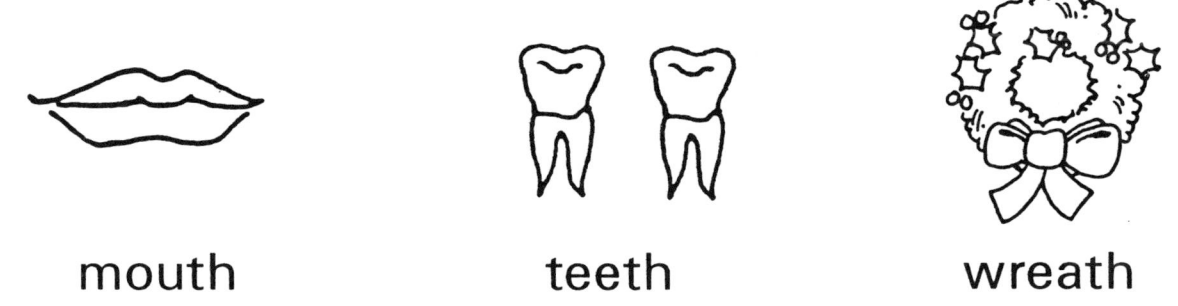

mouth   teeth   wreath

Say the name of each picture aloud.

Cut out all the squares and paste each one in the center of a 2½-inch cardboard square. Spread out the squares face down on a table. The object is to find matching pairs. One player turns over any two cards, and says, "This is a _____ and this is a _____." If the cards are alike, he removes them and takes another turn. If they are not alike, he turns them face down again and it becomes the next player's turn. The player with the most pairs wins.

three	three	tooth	tooth	thumb
thumbtack	thumbtack	toothbrush	toothbrush	thumb
thorn	thorn	thermos	thermos	thread
mouth	mouth	feather	feather	thread

Speech Improvement
Reproducible Masters (Revised)